How to Choose a Pet

Clare Chandler

Photo Credits

ZEFA, cover main image.

Oxford Scientific Films/Max Gibbs, cover top left, page 4 top left, page 6.

FLPA/J Bastable, page 5 top right.

Sally Anne Thompson, page 4 middle right, page 11 bottom, page 15 bottom, page 19 top right.

Thompson/Willbie Animal Photography, page 18 bottom left.

Willbie Animal Photography, page 19 bottom left.

Telegraph Colour Library/Carola Bayer, page 20 bottom.

Planet Earth Pictures/Doug Perrine, page 21 bottom.

Photomax, goldfish equipment, page 22 bottom.

All other photographs, Trevor Clifford.

Illustrations

All illustrations by Oxford Illustrators

We recommend that you consult a specific book on each animal before choosing or buying any pet.

Discovery World:

How to Choose a Pet

©1998 Rigby
a division of Reed Elsevier Inc.
1000 Hart Road
Barrington, IL 60010-2627

02 01
10 9 8

Printed in the United States of America
ISBN 0-7635-2355-0

Visit Rigby's Education Station® on the World Wide Web at http://www.rigby.com

Contents

Rigby

Choosing Your Pet

It is very exciting to get a pet. It is a new friend to play with, but it will need taking care of.

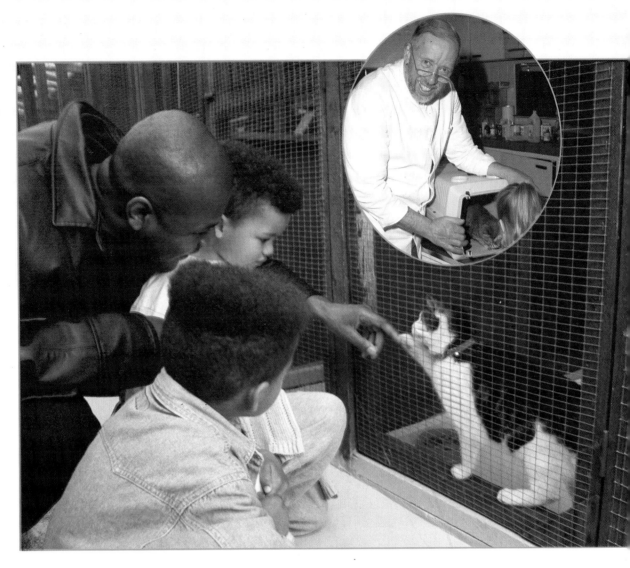

A vet may know of an animal that needs a home. You can also get a pet from an animal shelter. You can buy a pet from a pet shop or from private owners or breeders.

This book gives you information about six different animals. It will help you to decide which pet you could best take care of.

Goldfish

A goldfish is easy to take care of.

Home

A goldfish needs

- to live in a tank with clean, fresh water
- places to hide, like rocks and plants
- to live with other goldfish

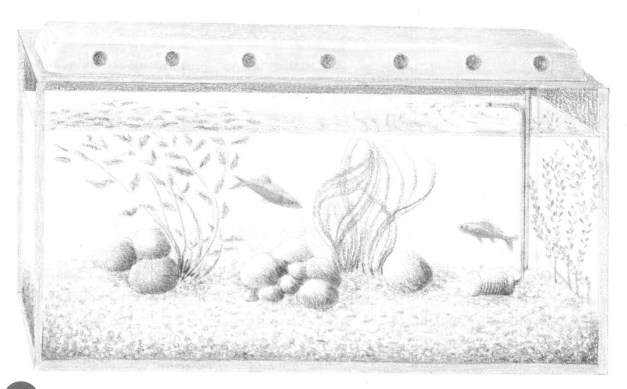

Food

A goldfish needs

- fish flakes, every day

- frozen worms or food tablets once a week

Care

Remember to

- change some of the water in the tank once every two weeks

- use a net, not your hands, to take out your goldfish

Hamster

A hamster is fun to watch while it plays.

Home

A hamster needs

- a large cage
- shredded plain paper or hay for bedding
- places to exercise, like ladders and wheels

Food

Every day, a hamster needs

- fresh fruit and vegetables
- hamster food
- clean, fresh water

Care

Remember to

- clean out the cage once a week
- be careful when you pick up your hamster or it may bite you

Guinea Pig

A guinea pig is furry and friendly.

Home

A guinea pig needs

- a hutch with two rooms, one small for sleeping
- shredded plain paper or hay for bedding
- a safe place to play in every day

Food

Every day, a guinea pig needs

- guinea pig food, fresh fruit, and vegetables
- grass and leaves
- clean, fresh water

Care

Remember to

- clean out the hutch one or two times a week
- let your guinea pig have lots of exercise
- handle your guinea pig gently

Rabbit

Rabbits come in all
shapes and sizes.

Home

A rabbit needs

- a large, warm hutch with two rooms
- wood shavings or straw for bedding
- a safe place to play in every day

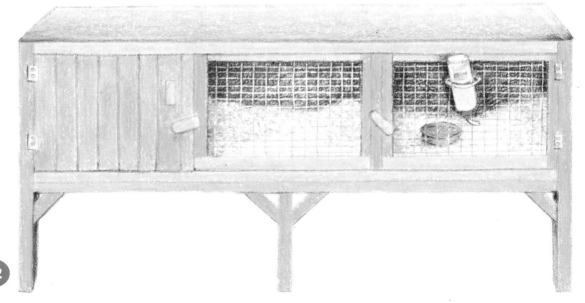

Food

Every day, a rabbit needs

- a mixture of oats, wheat, and rabbit pellets

- fresh fruit and vegetables

- hay

- clean, fresh water

Care

Remember to

- clean out the hutch two or three times a week

- brush your rabbit if it has long hair

Cat

A cat likes to play and also likes time to itself.

Home

A cat needs

- a warm, cozy place to sleep
- somewhere to sharpen its claws
- lots of space to run around

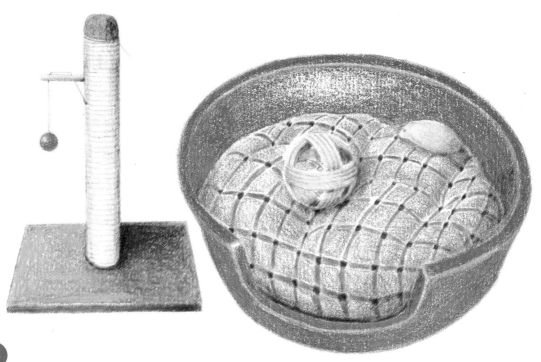

Food

Every day, a cat needs

- canned or dry cat food
- clean, fresh water

Care

Remember to

- train your cat to use a litter box
- take your cat to the vet for regular injections

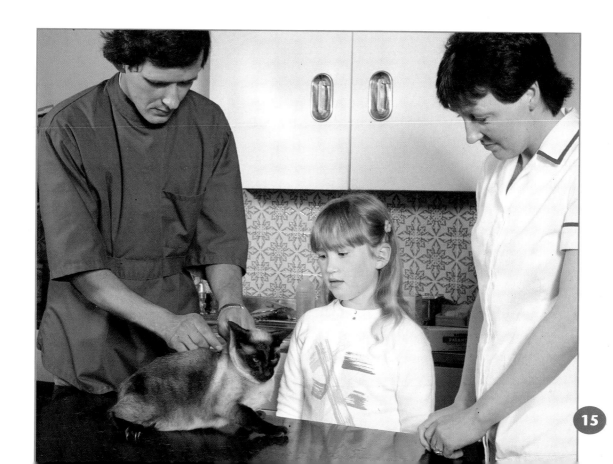

Dog

A dog can be a very
good friend.

Home

A dog needs

- a warm bed with a blanket

- not to be left on its own for too long

- lots of space to run around

- toys and things to chew

Food

Every day, a dog needs:

- canned and dry dog food

- clean, fresh water

Care

Remember to

- walk your dog every day for exercise

- clean up after your dog

- take your dog to the vet for regular injections

- train your dog to be well-behaved

Caring for a Pet

Before you choose a pet, think about how much care it will need. These are some questions you should think about.

Will your pet need a place to exercise?

Yes	No

Can its home be outdoors?

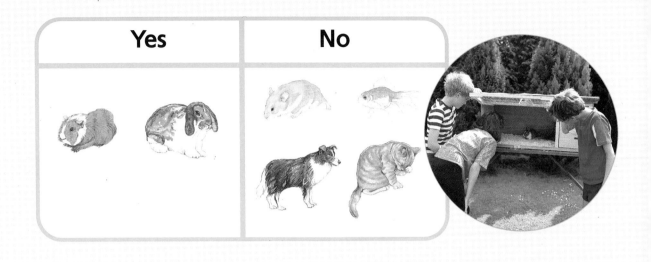

Yes	No

Will you need to clean out its home often?

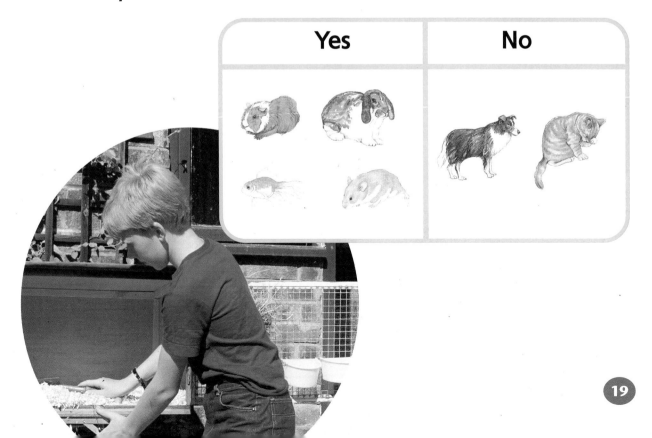

Yes	No

Will you need to brush your pet?

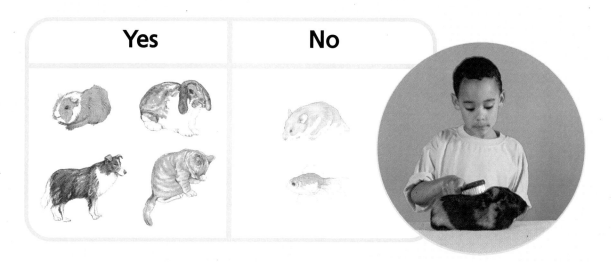

Yes	No

Will you need to play with your pet often?

Yes	No

All pets need care and love. Some pets need more attention than others. Some cost more to keep. Which pet could you take care of?

If you cannot have a pet in your home, you could

○ adopt an animal in a zoo

○ help a wild animal in danger by sponsoring a seal, a gorilla, or even a whale!

Getting Ready for Your Pet

When you have chosen your pet, try to have things ready for it when it arrives.

Buy or borrow a book about your pet. Find out the address of a vet near you. Your pet may need injections.

Make a list of all the things your pet will need. Make sure you have everything ready.

Amazing Pet Facts

A pet rabbit can have as many as 72 babies in one year!

A goldfish, named Fred, lived until he was 41 years old!

The smallest cat ever, named Tinker Toy, was about 3 inches tall!

a b c d e f g h i j k l m n o p q r s t u v w x y z

Index